Selling to the Seven Emotional Buying Styles

Make Every Sales Call Pay by Selling to Emotional Needs

Greg Ferrett

Exceptional Sales Performance

Disclaimer

While every precaution has been taken in the preparation of this publication, the authors assume no responsibility for errors or omissions. Neither is any liability assumed for damages resulting from the use of the information contained therein.

National Library of Australia
Cataloguing-in-Publication entry

Ferrett, Gregory, 1954 –
Selling to the Seven Emotional Buying Styles: Make Every Sales Call Pay by Selling to Emotional Needs / Gregory Ferrett
Bibliography
Includes index
ISBN 978 0 9873729 0 1
Selling
Selling – Handbooks, manuals, etc.
Selling – Vocational guidance

Dewey 658.85

Published by Exceptional Sales Performance
Cheltenham, Victoria, Australia 3129

You see things; and you say "Why?"
But I dream things that never were; and I say "Why not?"

George Bernard Shaw

Acknowledgements

Thankyou to the team of people who helped me work on this book and make it happen.

To Michael Tregonning who introduced me to Emotional Styles through the game 'The Gatekeepers™', the science behind Emotional Intelligence and helped in the development of the text. To my forum group at National Speakers who helped me come up with the title and first encouraged me to compile this book. Also to the hundreds of individuals I have mentored and coached who listened to my ideas as I developed the concepts in this book

The stories used in this book are all taken from my professional experience in sales and coaching sales professionals and new business start-ups. In some cases the names of the companies and individuals have been changed to protect the identity of the individual.

Brenda Brown is the genius who saw the humour in each Emotional Style and created the cartoons.

Steven Peterson is the brilliant mind behind the cover design. He took my message and created the visual interpretation you see here. Also to my family, and especially my son Joel, a professional editor and writer, who helped with all aspects of getting this manuscript ready for publication.

About the author

Greg works with people where influencing others decisions and their behaviour is critical to their success and is a highly regarded sales and business coach. He is CEO of Exceptional Sales Performance (ESP) based in Melbourne, Australia and provides coaching, training and consulting services throughout Asia Pacific – this book is testament to his approach.

Greg is a student of the sciences unlocking the complexities of human behaviour and what drives people to make decisions. He takes the complexities of these new understandings and provides everyday tools allowing people he works with to easily and quickly establish connections with others based on trust. Using these tools he helps them become superior performers and people of influence in everything they do.

One of Greg's specialities is business start-up and business turnaround coaching where he has helped many people build profitable businesses from first principles and rescue businesses in trouble.

Greg's passion is people. He helps them achieve what they never thought was possible. This book brings out a lifetime of business and sales experience and provides you with examples of how to apply his experience with emotional intelligence to improve your sales skills and your life.

Greg takes a very practical approach and uses experiences working with global services organizations and brand new enterprises. He has coached partners at PricewaterhouseCoopers; Consulted to major systems integrators such as Samsung SDS; Developed and delivered programs for global telecommunications companies such as LINK Communications & Genesys Conferencing. He has experience in engineering, skin care, FMCG, medical, boutique retail, IT development, business process outsourcing and more. Greg has supported and coached sales professionals, consultants and partners with career defining results.

Make every sales call pay by applying the principals in this book.

For further information on Greg visit

http://www.exceptionalsales.com.au

Table of Contents

CHAPTER 1

OVERVIEW

Since the first human being made a decision scientists and philosophers have expended enormous amounts of time and effort determining what goes on in the brain as a decision point is reached.

Until recently the brain was a mystery, a 'black box', and understanding of the way the brain made decisions was based on observation rather than science. When a decision is made it was assumed the human brain weighs up the facts and determines a logical solution. Over time this ability to think logically became what defined us as humans.

In his book *How We Decide* Jonah Lehrer[1] uses the example of Lieutenant Commander Michael Riley, a radar operator during the first Iraq war. He was monitoring an unknown blip heading straight for the USS Missouri and 550 sailors. The blip looked like a friendly A-6 returning from action; however, there was no electronic identification. The blip was travelling the same course and speed he expected an A-6 returning from action to follow. For some reason, despite the logical evidence, Riley was certain it was an Iraqi surface to air missile and issued the order to fire. Two sea dart surface-to-air missiles were launched to destroy the object. Was it an A-6 returning from a sortie? Or was it a hostile missile heading towards the USS Missouri?

It turned out the object was a hostile missile and Riley had saved the

---

1   *How We Decide*, Lehrer, Jonah 2009 Houghton Mifflin Harcourt

lives of 550 sailors that day. Was he just lucky? Or was something else at work? Riley had subconsciously seen an anomaly which gave him a 'gut feeling' something was wrong and he acted on that. If he had hesitated and acted on logic the lives of every sailor on the USS Missouri would have been lost.

When you make a decision your body is under stress and your brain is awash with chemicals driving emotion. The same thing happens with your client and every person involved in making a decision to buy. Your client may claim they are making a rational decision totally based on logic. No matter how loud they protest if their green or red emotional buttons are being pushed emotion will drive them. You and your client may not even be aware of what is happening. The long held assumption about people being rational is just plain wrong.

Harvard Business School announced *The End of Solution Sales*[2] in July 2012. In their research covering more than 1,400 Business to Business customers they found, on average, nearly 60% of a purchasing decision is now made before even having the first conversation with a supplier. In fact, the research shows a sales rep can now be more of a hindrance than an asset and customers are way ahead of the salespeople trying to help them. The same research shows there are a small number of superior sales professionals who have changed the way they sell. This book addresses a fundamental aspect of this change – emotion.

Making a decision to buy, on the surface, appears to be a simple straightforward act so doing the research before getting a salesperson involved seems to make sense. Who else knows the customer better than the customer?

Under the surface, behind all the research and facts, your client is still a human being and will be experiencing a range of emotions – many which are out of their control. Your client is trying to sort out (consciously or sub-consciously) who they are comfortable doing business with and who they can trust to deliver the outcome they require. A critical part of today's

---

2   *The End of Solution Selling*, Adamson, Dixon and Toman- Harvard Business Review July 2012

selling process is helping your customer sort out their relationship with you and your organisation.

The number one rule in understanding business to business relationships is;

"A relationship can only be between two people – never between companies."

All other rules fall under this. While you can entertain and put on activities with many people, when it comes to business to business relationships, positive or negative each person working with your customer will measure you and your company on the individual relationship they have with your people. This relationship is measured emotionally and is their perception of the relationship they have with you or an individual in your company. Every activity you do with your client must reflect the nature of this relationship and the emotional needs of the individuals within your client.

Business to business relationships, positive or negative, stand on the emotional attachment an individual has with another individual.

In this book we explore a buyer's emotional drivers, or what I call emotional DNA. We will examine what makes up their emotional needs and how this will determine if they will make a decision to buy, and then if they will buy from you.

How powerful is emotion?

Since the turn of the century there has been a fundamental shift in our understanding of the importance and impact of emotion on an individual's decision making and the chemical makeup of their body. Recent pioneering research has been done on how the chemicals inside our bodies form a dynamic information network, linking our mind and body and establishing the bimolecular basis for our emotions. What this study has done is to provide understanding and scientific evidence of the powerful link between emotion and behaviour.

- Why do we feel the way we feel?
- How do our thoughts and emotions affect our health?

13

- Are our body and mind distinct from each other or do they function together as parts of an interconnected system?

What the study tells us is once your client's emotion is aroused (positive or negative) their biochemical system goes to work and starts to drive physical behaviour. Even if they appear to be 'detached' on the surface, once rapport is established there are powerful chemical influences at work in your clients body subconsciously moving them to a particular behaviour.

This is best understood by recent research which has unlocked the 'black box' of the brain to reveal how the brain makes decisions.

The brain has two main regions. The Neo-cortex and Limbic brain.

Neo-Cortex

This is the top layer of the cerebral hemispheres and is typically only a few millimetres thick. It has deep groves and wrinkles and is involved in higher functions. This layer of the brain gives you the ability to speak, to process complex thoughts, process spreadsheets and logically compare information to allow you to present ideas in a clinical way.

Limbic Brain

While there are many parts in this section of the brain, the remainder of the brain is generally referred to as the Limbic brain and is often referred to as the 'emotional brain' as it is here where emotions come from. While there is some debate on the details, in practical terms almost every decision you make is made in this part of the brain. This is where your 'gut feeling' comes from; where pictures and sound are processed. Most importantly this is all done without words as there is no capacity for language.

It is the limbic brain which is directly connected to the chemistry of your body and produces responses such as 'fight or flight' reactions. It is in this section of the brain where you will fall in love with that new car you just have to have, and then the Neo-Cortex takes over to justify the expense.

When an emotion is triggered in the limbic brain, good or bad, it starts a chemical reaction which automatically produces a strong reaction in you

14

which, once triggered, is difficult to control. Often you will hear people who have done something crazy say things like 'I just couldn't stop myself'. This is the limbic brain producing a chemical reaction in response to an emotional trigger forcing them into action.

When you understand what triggers emotions in your own brain, you can start to understand the triggers in your client as well. When you understand them you can plan activities that trigger their emotions to make a powerful call to action.

In this book I will examine the seven emotional drivers, what I call the emotional DNA or Emnome, the emotional equivalent of the Genome. The Emnome is the total emotional makeup of an individual. The seven emotional building blocks this book introduces are present in every person. Understanding the complex makeup of the Emnome allows you to address the emotional needs of the individual you are selling to.

I will help you identify and plan activities to match the Emotional Style of your client. I will examine activities which you can use to push your clients green button and help you avoid activities that push their red button.

Commercial relationships and emotion

Every sale, in the end, is a result of two human beings sitting down and agreeing to move forward with a joint solution. Your client engages you to deliver a business result because they trust you to deliver on your word – and this is because of the trust they have in the relationship they have with you. Real commercial relationships are honest, sincere, of value and meaning to both parties.

Each individual in a commercial relationship will have a different emotional makeup that must be satisfied before forming a longer-term relationship.

I and others have learnt from foundations originally laid down by Aaron Rosanoff in his work on personality needs in the 1920's. Later this was further developed by Humm-Wadsworth. In 1935 he mapped these emotional needs and established a Temperament Scale based on Rosanoff's theory of personality needs.

Over the past twenty years, my colleagues and I have developed a lasting appreciation of this work and realised how this scientific base has an equally effective application in sales.[3]

Once you know your client's Emnome or emotional make-up, you can establish individual plans to meet their emotional needs. The client relationship fed on a strong foundation of consistent, varied, and sincere emotional food has less of a chance of being forgotten when someone new comes along or happens to be the last one in the door.

Emotional buying styles or emotional genes

In their paper *The End of Solution Selling* Harvard Business School identifies a core strategy of targeting mobilisers, not advocates. They identify seven profiles of people which roughly map into the seven emotional genes.

These are the seven primary Emotional Styles or emotional genes. For each Emotional Style, I would suggest there is a green and red button you can push to open up the buyers sense of;

- Pain or Pleasure
- Inadequacy or Capability
- Deprivation or Plenty

Push the wrong button(s) and you are in for a long and frustrating sales campaign.

If you ignore these emotional drivers and deal with your clients using your own emotional drivers you risk pushing the wrong button six out of seven times!

---

3   A historical survey of personality scales and inventories- Lewis R. Goldberg 1971

The seven emotional buying styles are now typically referred to as:

- Normal
- Hustler
- Mover
- Double Checker
- Artist
- Politician
- Engineer

In this book I will introduce you to each style and their unique characteristics and expressions. We will look at the complexities of the Emnome or emotional genome and how these Emotional Styles often play out in real life.

Determining the Emotional Make Up

This book will provide you with tools so you can pick these seven styles by their actions, the words they use, their appearance and other simple tools. Often, when I am sitting in a reception area waiting for my appointment I observe people that pass by and predict their primary Emotional Style. It is fun and it is profitable.

It is important to remember that while a person is likely to have a primary Emotional Style, the Emnome or emotional make-up is complex and most people will have at least a little of all seven styles. Understanding this mix is vital in developing a longer term strategy to build a relationship.

This book deals primarily with selling to people by understanding the emotional make-up of an individual and addressing the emotional needs of the individual. With the right training and a desire to practice your art, you will be able to identify your customer's primary Emotional Style and consequent buying behaviour. When you understand this you can sell in a way that satisfies this emotional need – and mobilise your customers to action..

CHAPTER 2

DISCOVERY OF THE EMNOME OR EMOTIONAL STYLES

Paul, the divisional president of Australia's largest telecommunications organisation, was a difficult client. I recall one particular sales call and the stress I felt as I debriefed with my sales manager after the call. No matter what sales technique I had tried there was no way Paul was going to budge. Every time I tried to move the sale forward with a question or trial close he would just sit there quietly with a strange smile on his face, say as few words as possible, as I slowly agreed to his every point. In the end I finally caved in on price (with a big reduction in commission) in the hope a deal could be struck and we would finally reach a conclusion.

Ken was Paul's counterpart in the 'user' community of this organisation. While he had some influence the decision was always going to be with Paul. I shared my experience with Ken and he let me in on a secret. Paul was regarded as one of the sharpest negotiators in the organisation with a reputation for getting deals through when no one else could. Ken coached me to restructure my offering in a way that reinforced Paul's reputation of getting things others could not.

I had followed a conservative solution selling strategy as this appeared to be what the organisation wanted. What I decided to do was to test out an idea. I decided to introduce a new product I thought may add to Paul's reputation and something I could achieve with a bit of sharp manoeuvring.

To achieve this I asked a simple question, "Paul, if your division could be the first organisation outside the US to implement this new technology, without increasing the price above the initial estimate, would that allow you to achieve your goal of staff time to productivity?"

I watched his face, and for the first time I saw a flicker of life. I was on to a winner. He composed himself and asked in his normal dry tone of voice "Could you do that?"

With the use of a single question I had turned an opportunity around and accidentally stumbled onto the secret of motivating buyers using emotion.

A few years later I sat in on a sales call with one of my team. This particular prospect had proved difficult to close and had put off making a decision a number of times. I listened to the sales pitch he was using, telling the prospect how they could become an innovator and take a leadership position in their market. Our prospect was starting to breathe more shallowly and began pushing back. We were losing him.

I looked on his wall and saw degrees and certificates from six different organisations. On his shelf he had every product catalogue for the past seven years from every supplier – in order. I realised we were most likely dealing with the Normal Emotional Style.

With an understanding of his likely emotional green buttons I took control and said "Eugene, I understand this is a big step for your organisation. This product is used by the top organisations in your field in North America and based on research we had commissioned by an independent research company in Australia will produce even better results here. Just authorise us to do this work and we will put the equipment in place and if it does not meet the benchmarks we proposed within three months we will come and take it back at no charge."

The whole mood changed. We had stopped pushing his red button and pushed his green button.

What I had done was to understand the buyers emotional DNA and used that knowledge to immediately change the energy in the room from negative (pushing red buttons) to positive (pushing green buttons). This changed the course of the sale. Their emotional DNA had wired up certain green and red buttons ready to be pushed – and we had been pushing all the red ones. Now we were pushing only green buttons and addressing the nutritional requirements of his emotional DNA.

What is emotional DNA?

Physicist Erwin Schrödinger, in his classic 1944 book *What is Life?* presents the idea that life is based on molecules and most physical laws on a large scale (such as the human body) are due to random actions of molecules on a small scale. As the number of atoms is reduced the system behaves more and more randomly. At the same time life, by and large, depends on order. By following these two thoughts it could be argued that logic dictates the master code of life and must consist of a large number of atoms.

The reality is not so and Schrödinger calls this principle order-from-disorder. At a fundamental level the blueprint of life is based on a few clearly defined molecules.

James D. Watson, in his memoir *DNA, The Secret of Life* credited *What is Life?* as his inspiration to research the gene, which led to the discovery of the DNA double helix structure. While DNA has many complexities, it is fundamentally constructed on just four clearly defined molecules called Nucleotides:

- Adenine
- Thiamine
- Guanine
- Cytosine

The scientific world has buzzed with excitement for nearly seventy years as money poured into genetic research. The search for the magic elixir, a pill or medical procedure that could fix everything was on. Even today this search continues despite growing evidence DNA, while important, is now considered a starting point and there may be more fundamental things controlling the chemistry of our body and our life.

I still find research about DNA and the chemistry of the body interesting. However, what captures my mind are some of the more exciting scientific studies today that show the link between the mind and body – and how the mind can control the chemistry of the body. There have been a number of 'out there' experiments where it is claimed DNA, the blueprint of life, can be manipulated purely by thought. In his book *The Biology of Belief*[4] Bruce Lipton examines stunning scientific evidence about how the mind affects the cells in your body at an atomic level.

This is not at all surprising as philosophers and religious leaders since Plato have observed and taught this as a fundamental part of life. In fact the evidence for this link has been around since the first human walked the earth. "What the mind of man can conceive and believe, it can achieve", attributed to Napoleon Hill in his book *Think and Grow Rich* is one of the most often used quotes by motivational speakers today. In a world dominated by a need for hard scientific evidence (almost the opposite as in the days of Galileo) philosophical evidence is often discounted. Hard scientific evidence is now emerging about the link between mind and body.

---

4   *The Biology of Belief – unleashing the Power of Consciousness, Matter & Miracles,* 2005, Lipton, Bruce

Quotes about Belief and Behaviour

"I tell you the truth, if you have faith as small as a mustard seed, you can say to this mountain, "Move from here to there" and it will move". - Jesus Christ

"One comes to believe whatever one repeats to oneself sufficiently often, whether the statement be true or false. It comes to be the dominating thought in one's mind." - Robert Collier

"It is a man's own mind, not his enemy or foe that lures him to evil ways" - Buddha

"What we can or cannot do, what we consider possible or impossible, is rarely a function of our true capability. It is more likely a function of our beliefs about who we are." - Anthony Robbins

"Do or do not ... there is no try" – Yoda, fictional character from Star Wars

Today these philosophical quotations are being brought to centre stage through rigorous scientific experimentation. The evidence from these studies is there is something more fundamental that drives human behaviour – even more than genetics – and that is emotion. The seven emotional styles or emotional genes are the equivalent to the nucleotides that build up DNA. Emotion and belief is the DNA of life, the driver of everyday behaviour. When we examine emotion and belief, just as in examining DNA, we discover there are only a few building blocks on which the fabric of human behaviour is built. The emotional make up of the individual is made up of a complex array of these emotional styles or emotional genes. This emotional make up is what I call the Emnome.

CHAPTER 3

UNDERSTANDING THE SEVEN EMOTIONAL STYLES

You have met with a new prospect and uncovered a potential opportunity. Your product or service meets their needs exactly and you have done all the things you normally do to establish a relationship. For some reason, however, you just can't seem to move into rapport. No matter what you do you seem to be pushing your prospects 'red button' and they are moving further away.

What is likely to be happening is you are not addressing your prospects basic human need – to be dealt with on an emotional level. Each individual is a human being and they have their own emotional DNA. For each emotional need there is a green and red button. By pushing the same buttons with every prospect you will be pushing a lot or red buttons and you may be spending a lot of time pushing buttons that are not even wired up!

How can we know which buttons to push or not push? Which ones are working and which ones is a waste of time?

In this and following chapters we will examine the fundamental building blocks of belief, the seven Emotional Styles, describe these Emotional Styles, provide case studies to help you understand which Emotional Styles the person you are dealing with has, what their red and green buttons are, and how to communicate and sell to each one.

Emotion Drives Everything

In every decision a business makes there is always a human being involved – and as a consequence emotion is involved in every decision.

Abraham Maslow observed each of us is motivated by basic human needs. These needs are born in us having evolved over millions of years. Maslow developed a hierarchy of needs to help explain how these needs motivate us all starting with the basic need for survival.

Physiological needs -	air, food, drink, shelter, warmth, sex, sleep
Safety needs -	protection from elements, security, order, law, limits, stability
Belongingness, Love & Affection needs -	work, family, affection, relationships
Esteem needs -	self-esteem, achievement, mastery, independence, status, dominance, prestige, managerial responsibility
Self-Actualization needs -	realising personal potential, self-fulfilment, seeking personal growth and peak experiences.

According to Maslow a person will only focus on the higher level of need where the lower level of need is satisfied. Only when the lower order needs of physical and emotional well-being are satisfied are we concerned with the higher order needs of influence and personal development. Conversely, if our lower order needs are no longer met, we are no longer concerned about the maintaining of our higher order needs.

What is interesting about Maslow's hierarchy is that if we know the emotional DNA or style of an individual experiencing pressure or achievement at each level we can predict reasonably accurately how that person will respond to the pressure or achievement of each level of Maslow's model.

In one Emotional Style a person will respond in a diplomatic way when their emotional need is met – yet in a manipulative way when under pressure or their emotional need is not satisfied. In the same circumstances another Emotional Style will spend a lot of time weighing up the facts and make good decisions, yet when their emotional needs are challenged they make snap judgements.

A 2004 study estimated Australians spent $10.5 billion, in one year, on items that they never actually used. Similar research in 2010 showed Australian families gave more than $1.1 billion in Christmas gifts that were either immediately thrown away or never used.

The reason humans are so wasteful is emotion drives the decision to purchase.

This is not just a phenomenon in households. The same happens in business. One of my consulting clients invested over $500 million in software licences and application development before making the decision never to turn on the system! This was an emotional decision by the CEO and imposed on the organisation. This is not an isolated incident with individuals in businesses making purchasing decisions regularly on an emotional basis and never using the product or service.

Emotion, the energy that drives all decisions, is being understood more clearly as dozens of studies show the way emotion drives every aspect of human behaviour. Every decision is made as a response to emotional needs or the Emnome – and the Emnome is made up of combinations of only seven Emotional Styles or emotional genes. When a purchasing or buying decision is made the decision is an emotional response to a well executed presentation/sale or sales campaign.

Aren't Buying Decisions Made On Logic?

If I lost a sale I would dread telling my sales manager the deal was lost. The first question was always 'Why?' Of course there was always a reason why a sale was lost – price, function or some other reason.

I have attended many lost sale analysis meetings. The end result of each of these meetings is the production of a list of logical reasons why a sale

27

was lost. I recall one such meeting where our client was invited to attend and detail the reasons why they had made a particular decision. The client produced a long list of reasons why they made the decision. This included price, ability to deliver on time, project team members – and in the end it was very clear why they had made the logical decision. My observation was they had outlined exactly the same reasons why another, very similar, client had purchased the same service from me using the same people at the same price – and the company they had rejected was the one we had just lost to with this prospect. How can you win and lose for the same reasons?

When I asked the question, "At what stage did you realise that you were probably going to purchase from our competitor?" They said, "When we realised we could get moving without the need to fully detail what we were trying to do". There it was! They had made an emotional decision and had gone through the motions to get board level approval. In this particular organisation they had the Hustler Emotional Style as the decision maker – while the company we had won the business with had the Normal Emotional Style in charge. They had the same logical needs but very different emotional requirements. If we had understood this we could easily have changed strategy and won both projects.

From the moment our prospect had engaged emotionally with our competitors the only sales activity of value we could have engaged in was to break that emotional link and establish an emotional link to us – but we had focused on the logic and sold as if we were selling to the Normal Emotional Style.

No matter how logical or illogical it may seem, if you are responsible for helping clients make a decision to buy from you it is your responsibility to identify the Emotional Style of each individual on the client team – which will help establish their buying style. By understanding the Emotional Style of your client you can uncover their green and red buttons allowing you to establish emotional links and break emotional links to competitors.

The Seven Emotional Styles

When you deal with decision makers there is a strong tendency to assume that LOGIC will carry the day. You believe in your product or service so just tell them what it does and everyone will buy. Simple, isn't it.

As the Harvard Business School study shows us, by the time your prospect engages with you more than 60% of the logical decision making process is already done with. Once you engage with a prospect it is important to understand the logic and address this. It is more important to understand the emotion.

I want to turn our attention now to how to attach each logical decision to an emotional need, and then address the emotional need.

The seven Emotional Styles or emotional genes are commonly referred to as:

- Normal
- Hustler
- Mover
- Double Checker
- Artist
- Politician
- Engineer

As I introduce each style, please do not start to link a job title to an individuals Emnome or emotional makeup. It is easy to look at a city like Washington or Canberra and assume they are full of people with the Politician emotional gene. Just because someone is labelled a politician does not mean their dominant Emotional Style is the Politician. They have a complex emotional makeup and often a person behind the politician is providing the political emotional agenda. You need to understand and address the individual's emotional needs.

Selling to each style

While I could take any number of examples to illustrate the point, for the purposes of this book I will simply use one example to make the point.

As I introduce each style, and their Emotional Style, I will use the example of a Real Estate agent attempting to sell a property that has one distinguishing and outstanding feature. In our example it is the rear timber decking or deck.

While I will take this simplistic approach, remember the emotional makeup or Emnome of your prospect will almost always be more complex. Understanding the complexity will allow you to more effectively sell to the individual.

Stress

One major advantage a sales person has in understanding and addressing the emotional needs of an individual is the primary emotional driver will come to the forefront at a time of stress. When a person is in decision making mode they are under stress. This means the primary emotional driver will become more obvious and, at the same time, become more dominant in their response to your proposal. This makes it easier to understand and address the emotional needs of the buyer.

CHAPTER **4**

NORMAL EMOTIONAL STYLE

The Normal Emotional Style will have a very conservative or formal manner about them. They will not respond easily to small talk nor will they reveal much about themselves. Most salespeople will find themselves slightly uncomfortable in their presence. The experienced salespeople will recognise this person straight away.

Their primary drive is for *social acceptance* and they are driven by a need to conform and function well within the social norms. Any suggestion of a deal or special discount will make them very uncomfortable as it may suggest something untoward.

Selling to the Normal

As I introduce each Emotional Style I am going to use a hypothetical example to illustrate how each style can respond positively to a specific product feature.

I will use the example of a Real Estate agent attempting to sell a property that has one distinguishing and outstanding feature, the rear timber decking or deck.

While this may seem simplistic, it allows me to illustrate how to position the feature in the terms of each Emotional Style. You need to remember the emotional makeup or Emnome of your prospect will almost always be more complex. Understanding the complexity will allow you to more effectively sell to the individual.

"Mr/Mrs/Ms Normal Emotional Style... This deck has full Council approval and it complies with all necessary building standards."

Why is this comment so relevant to closing the sale with the Normal Emotional Style? To many of us this would be superfluous and self-evident – something that is assumed. However, the reality is the Normal Emotional Style's sense of deprivation is most likely engendered when they are seen to be doing anything that even vaguely resembles something illegal or untoward. They crave *social acceptance* so strongly that they have never missed or reneged on a payment or financial commitment in their life.

In fact they have probably never had a speeding or parking ticket.

By taking the time to point out that the decking has full council approval you are taking the time to push the Normal Emotional Style's green button. When you ask a Normal Emotional Style to make a quick decision, offer a discount for a quick decision or suggest anything out of the 'normal' you will push their red button and find their response to you will change.

When you meet the Normal in business they are the ones that like detail. They will have everything on file. They tend to award smaller projects to a supplier before they are comfortable to award an entire job.

When you first meet them in their office you will probably notice they display their qualifications and other certificates of achievement. Their office is probably organised and work-oriented. Their demeanour is typically businesslike.

Working with the Normal

The Normal typically learns and communicates using pictures and words so communication needs to be clear and contain visual content. They like clear communication, clean offices and unambiguous instructions.

Your initial meeting

When you first meet the Normal they may appear uninterested or cool. You will need to be prepared with questions focusing on logic and process. Here are a few conversation starters to get the Normal going.

- How will you be handling the selection process for this role?
- What are the important aspects of the new program which need to fit into the current system?
- Why do you think the board behaved that way in the previous decision?
- Where will this make the biggest difference to you and your team?
- When do you see this happening?

Once you have established your credentials with the Normal they will start to use you as a sounding board so taking the time to get to know them, especially a person with a degree of influence, can yield big dividends. These are the people who will tell you who the likely road blocks to a decision will be and why.

As this is the first meeting you will want to avoid emotional questions. You can ask questions about qualifications and awards, especially if they are on display. Questions about their desire to improve themselves are also good ways to get the conversation going.

Avoid challenging the way things are being done and try something like, 'If you were going to improve on what you have now what would you do?'

Follow-up

The Normal appreciates written communication outlining the conversation and may even beat you to the punch. Keep in contact with them providing examples of your product and services working in similar environments. If your company wins an award, or has some good press, this will help build the relationship with the Normal.

Most importantly, if there are action points you promised to follow-up on make sure they happen when you said they would.

EMOTIONAL STYLE

	Green Button	Red Button
Normal	Examples of other success Offer guarantees Point out how your product or service is an established and recognised process	Criticise or challenge their integrity Offer special discounts or a deal outside normal terms Being late Avoiding an issue or being secretive

Normal Emotional Style

Primary Driver: Social Acceptance

What to look for		To communicate with	To present and Close them
Language	Logical, Rational, Formal, Unemotional & Precise	• Use formal courtesies throughout discussion	• Use "Narrative" style
		• Get to the point straight away	• Incorporate as many references as possible
Ideals	Professional	• Don't engage in small talk unless you are invited	• Never offer a discount or suggest a "Deal"
Vocation	Law, Aviation, Finance or Commerce	• Be even and unemotional in manner, dress and voice	• Mention other major companies that do business with you
Image	Conservative, Old school tie, Black, White & Gray	• Focus on solutions when criticising or presenting ideas	• Use a logical, formal, rational & planned format
Neatness	Orderly, Formal, Neat & tidy desk, Landscape or portrait of founder	• Praise when appropriate, however, do not overdo it	• Do cost / benefit analysis
Gambit	On time & Formal		• Offer guarantees

Emnome Worksheet

Consider the Normal Emotional Style. Identify a person in a current or past sales campaign who has influence on the sales outcome and which you think best summarises this Emotional Style. If there are others in your organisation who are involved with this person or campaign get them involved with this discussion as well.

Name :

Role :

What outward signs give you the clues about this person Emnome? You might want to use the LIVING table on page 91

1.

2.

3.

In dealing with this person have you pushed their green or red buttons? What happened?

_____

_____

_____

List three things you could do with this person to help build your relationship with them.

1.

2.

3.

CHAPTER 5

HUSTLER EMOTIONAL STYLE

The Hustler Emotional Style will have a far more outgoing and polished or slick manner about them. You may start to wonder who is selling who with this style of person. Are you selling them the house or are they trying to sell you on how successful they are.

Hustlers are notorious "name droppers." They are usually very well dressed and they have a strong tendency to display all the outward signs of material wealth. (Check out the car they are driving)

Their primary desire is for *material success* and all the trappings that go with it.

It doesn't mean they have achieved their goal but they will want you to think they have (The Mercedes in the driveway is probably leased).

They are the direct opposite to the Normal Emotional Style. They are driven to get a better or sharper deal than anyone else.

Selling to the Hustler

When it comes to the decking or deck...

"Mr/Mrs/Ms Hustler Emotional Style...This deck adds real prestige to the property. If you want to put a pergola over the top you might spend $10,000 extra but it would add $30,000 to the value of the property. Perhaps we could work this factor into your loan package and get it done straight away."

This style wants it all now. They don't worry about paying for it or what they can afford. It is purely a matter of how good it makes them look and whether it can be done quickly.

You may even find them coming up with solutions or alternatives you didn't think of.

If you can't sell this style it's completely your own fault. Cut to the chase; don't be boring, tedious or pedantic. If you are, you will lose them very quickly.

When you meet the Hustler in business they will be brisk and to the point. They will want the whole picture now, including your best price. To push their green button you need to be quick to get back to them, provide quality work rapidly and you will get on well with them. They will make decisions quickly without all the facts. Push their red button and they will categorise you as a loser and your proposal will languish at the bottom of the pack.

When you first meet them in their office you are likely to notice is it is set up to impress. The desk will be in a dominate position and their success will be on show.

Working with the Hustler

The Hustler typically learns and communicates using words and feelings so communication needs to combine the two.

Your initial meeting

You will have no trouble getting the Hustler into a conversation if you start talking about them and their success. You will need to plan the transition into selling mode or the whole appointment will be about the Hustler and how good they are and not your product of service.

Here are a few conversation starters to get the Hustler going.

- How important do you feel this role is?
- What do you feel are the two most important tasks to get this return?
- Why do you feel the board considers this important?
- Where will this make the biggest difference to you?
- When do you feel we can make the project happen?

When you ask a question the Hustler may jump in and start talking before you finish. It is your job to sort out the words telling you how important they are from what the real story is.

As this is the first meeting personal questions are important. Ask about anything obvious which shows they are important. 'That Lexus LFA in your car park … it must be great to feel the power as you cruise down the Freeway. Did you have to wait long to take delivery?' Ask questions about their ambitions and their role in the project.

When you challenge them with a 'No' you are likely to get excuses. It is probably better to nod you head to acknowledge you have listened and ask, 'Could something like … have produced a better result?'

Follow-up

The Hustler craves to show others how important they are. There is nothing like entertaining them in a classy restaurant or a member's only club. If you can introduce them to a celebrity or well regarded business guru your standing with them will go forward in leaps and bounds.

Document everything with the Hustler. They will remember every conversation their own way and this recollection will change to suit their current circumstances. When there is a point of agreement make sure you say, 'No worries, I will document that so we can get moving straight away' and do it before the next opportunity comes along.

The hustler loves good surprises. If you call in and say, "I have this rare wine I want you to taste", they will remember you forever, or at least till the next opportunity to gain social standing comes along.

EMOTIONAL STYLE

	Green Button	Red Button
Hustler	Explain how they will have a personal win or advantage Compliment them on their achievements (be impressed) Get to the deal quickly while remaining concise	Sloppy appearance or unprofessional attitude Ignoring or not acknowledging their achievements

43

Hustler Emotional Style

Primary Driver: Desire for Material Success

What to look for		To communicate with	To present and Close them
Language	Talks money early, Good eye contact, Name dropper, Charming	• Praise should focus on enhancing their image	• Remember the "WIFM" (*What's in it for me*)
Ideals	Middleman	• Respond quickly if you need to be critical (*Tomorrow will be too late*)	• Close on discount (*Inducement*). A once only deal
Vocation	Broker, Sales, Changes jobs	• Be blunt when criticising and indicate loss of image	• Feed their ego (*Be impresses when they name drop*)
Image	Well groomed, Flashy gold accessories, Red	• Set clear goals and standards. Support with documentation	• Take them to lunch (*Expensive/ Prestigious*)
Neatness	Lavish or glitzy, Awards & prizes, Entertainment area	• Breakdown major projects into easily achieved short exercises	• Present yourself as a winner
Gambit	On time & Informal	• Listen attentively while ignoring excuses	• Do not be late for your appointment (*If you are late, you won't get the sale*)
			• Talk about the win/win

45

Emnome Worksheet

Consider the Hustler Emotional Style. Identify a person in a current or past sales campaign who has influence on the sales outcome and which you think best summarises this Emotional Style. If there are others in your organisation who are involved with this person or campaign get them involved with this discussion as well.

Name :

Role :

What outward signs give you the clues about this person Emnome? You might want to use the LIVING table on page 91

1.

2.

3.

In dealing with this person have you pushed their green or red buttons? What happened?

_____

_____

_____

List three things you could do with this person to help build your relationship with them.

1.

2.

3.

CHAPTER 6

MOVER EMOTIONAL STYLE

The Mover Emotional Style will also have a very outgoing manner about them. The first indication of this style will be that they will probably be late for the appointment and your conversation will invariably be interrupted by their mobile phone.

Their primary desire is to *communicate*. Although those that know this style intimately will tell you they just talk too much. This style has an overriding desire for social intercourse, they don't care who they are talking to just as long as they are breathing. Hence the overwhelming need for them to take that mobile phone call even when what they are doing should take all their attention. They can't help themselves.

Selling to the Mover

When it comes to the decking or deck...

"Mr/Mrs/Ms Mover Emotional Style... Look at the size of this deck. You could invite all your friends over for a BBQ and still have room for a dance floor and the Karaoke console."

The Mover Emotional Style is a good family man or women and if you get the chance to spot their car it will most likely be a "People Mover"

The Mover hates detail and you should offer to complete as much of the paper work as possible. If you suggest they turn off their mobile telephone or oblige them to do paperwork or search for details you will immediately push their red button. If you leave anything to them to do, it won't get done. To push their green button show them how your product or service will allow them to spend more time socialising and that you have all the details under control – just authorise this paperwork here.

When you meet the Mover Emotional Style in business you will immediately like them. They are warm, jovial and friendly and need to talk before getting down to business – if they ever do. If you have ever been involved in a sale where the initial meeting went so well you just 'knew' it was your deal – only to discover they have gone into a two year meeting – you know you have met a Mover.

When you first meet them in their office you will find their space to be open and friendly. They may have posters and personal items on their wall or desk. The desk will likely be messy and piled with things to do. Their demeanour is typically jovial.

Working with the Mover

The Mover typically learns and communicates using action and words. The first thing you notice with the Mover is they love to talk and often need to use their hands as well, as their mouth can't move fast enough to get the words out.

Your initial meeting

Getting a conversation going with the Mover is not a problem, once they turn up. It will be controlling the conversation where you are likely to have most problems. Here are a few conversation questions to keep the Mover under control.

- Tell me how you see your relationship with the person in this new role?
- Which departments will benefit most from this program?
- If you need specific information follow-up with 'How about HR?'
- What does the board feel about it?
- Who is making the most noise about this project?
- How do you see this happening?

When you ask a question the Mover is likely to be answering before you finish. When they talk about people they are likely to use emotional words and may even get emotional themselves. Just remain calm and listen.

Despite this being the first meeting the Mover will immediately treat you as their new best friend, call you by your first name and make you feel welcome. They will talk about others, including celebrities and board members, as if they have known them for years using their first name. You need to follow this pattern.

Enthusiasm and energetic conversation is what drives the Mover. To get detailed information you will need to ask specific questions to eke out the information and move on.

Follow-up

The Mover needs you to follow-up with the details and provide a specific action plan. If you ask for feedback to your action plan you are unlikely to get any. It is better to include a statement like, 'This is what we agreed. I will call next Friday to hear how you are doing on point 7.'

They respond well to humour, and love communication, so a hand written greeting card to thank them for the meeting with a funny or motivational message will go a long way to building the relationship.

Entertainment is also valued by the Mover. If you ask them to lunch, however, be prepared to spend the rest of the day with them.

EMOTIONAL STYLE

	Green Button	Red Button
Mover	Engage in conversation at their pace while checking regularly they have understood each of your points

Offer to get the paperwork done for them | Take away a choice

Negative words or phrases – especially picking up on missed details

Being dismissive of their ideas – no matter how silly or trivial they may be |

Mover Emotional Style

Primary Driver: Desire to Communicate

What to look for		To communicate with	To present and Close them
Language	Lively, laughter, Smiles, Jokes, Jumps topics	• Keep them focused on the topic or point. Do not accept generalisations, ask for details • Confirm action plans in writing • "Drop in" for an occasional chat	• Ask them to hold all calls & turn off mobile • Ask them to buy as many times as it takes • Use the "Order Form" close
Ideals	People	• Show how their actions either help or hurt people	• Use "Big Picture" stuff (*Movers hate details*)
Vocation	Sales, HR, Customer service	• Monitor their work volume and follow through	• Offer to process all forms involved (*if you leave it to them, it will never get done*)
Image	Tousled appearance, Fun colours, Casual, Collar undone & sleeves rolled up, Yellow	• Divide a long task into varied small tasks • Work best in a team environment	• Take them to lunch • Ask about family, friends and interests
Neatness	Messy desk, Bright & slogans on Wall		• Assumptive close
Gambit	Late & Informal		

53

Emnome Worksheet

Consider the Mover Emotional Style. Identify a person in a current or past sales campaign who has influence on the sales outcome and which you think best summarises this Emotional Style. If there are others in your organisation who are involved with this person or campaign get them involved with this discussion as well.

Name :

Role :

What outward signs give you the clues about this person Emnome? You might want to use the LIVING table on page 91

1.

2.

3.

In dealing with this person have you pushed their green or red buttons? What happened?

_____

_____

_____

List three things you could do with this person to help build your relationship with them.

1.

2.

3.

CHAPTER 7

DOUBLE CHECKER EMOTIONAL STYLE

The Double Checker Emotional Style will have a warm and accommodating manner about them rather than the outgoing nature of the Mover or Hustler. This kind and caring style is always a pleasure to deal with until it comes to the close or making a decision.

Their primary desire is for *security*. This person is often maligned by other styles as one who can't make a decision. The criticism is quite valid because they can't make decisions. What we need to know is why.

The reason is that the Double Checker Emotional Style sees what can go wrong long before they see anything else.

They also feel the impact of it even before or whether it happens. Basically, they are the epitome of the worrier. You may have heard the definition of worry before but I will repeat to demonstrate the point. "Worry is feeling the physical effect of something that has not actually happened."

The Double Checker will add one extra word to the above mentioned quote ... "Yet"

If you suspect you are dealing with this style just ask them how long they have been in their current job and you will have your suspicions confirmed when they tell you..."Years" They will tell you about all the problems they experience in their current role – but will not make a move for fear of what might happen in the new role.

The Double Checker will give up opportunity and material success for security. The public service is full of Double Checkers

Selling to the Double Checker

When it comes to the decking or deck...

"Mr/Mrs/Ms Double Checker... This deck has been put together by a very capable and qualified tradesman. It is fully reinforced, solid and built to last.

When you get to the close with this style you only have to remember a couple of rules.

By using the word 'Decision' you will push the Double Checkers red button. If you call to make an appointment to ask for a decision they are likely to be sick on the day. You need to take charge of the process and be the decision maker, the initiator. If you leave it up to them, you will be waiting a very long time.

Use reassuring language like "guarantee" and "safe".

Decide how much time you are prepared to spend/waste on this style.

If you have given it a good shot and they are still procrastinating, cut your losses and move on. It should not be a reflection on you as a sale person. Remember, this style hasn't done a lot in life because they have a genuine and overriding fear of failure.

Working with the Double Checker

The Double Checker typically learns and communicates using words and feeling so communication needs to be clear and often they need to experience the idea in operation. Use words and questions which prompt feelings.

Your initial meeting

The Double Checker may feel uncomfortable about your initial visit as they may feel their position challenged. You will need to indicate to the Double Checker you are visiting as their input is important and you need to hear their views. Here are a few conversation starters to get the Double Checker going.

- How is this role currently being handled?
- What do you feel the challenges are with the current program?
- Why do you think the board decided to move that way?
- Where do you feel the biggest improvements can be made?
- What do you feel may stand in the way of this happening?

When you ask a question pause and wait for the answer. The Double Checker may be acting out the situation in their mind and feeling the emotion.

The Double Checker may start to dump a lot of emotional baggage on you as they answer questions. You need to listen patiently, and reflect the answers back to them without the emotion to be sure you are getting the right story.

You can encourage the Double Checker by saying things like, 'This is really good information and will help immensely.'

Criticising or challenging the Double Checker can lead to unpredictable responses. If you want to get them onside you could say something like, "You seem to know the situation well. Perhaps we could work on the best solution together."

If the Double Checker becomes too negative you may need to redirect the conversation. You could try something like, "Yes that is certainly a problem. How might you have handled it?"

Follow-up

The Double Checker may have a warm demeanour; however they tend to lack initiative. They will not appreciate long lists of 'to-do' action points, so your follow-up needs to focus on tasks they can do quickly and well. The idea is to get them moving.

Early follow-up is important, adding new items to their 'to-do' list to maintain momentum towards the sales goal. If you leave follow-up too long they will get bogged down with all the other problems of the organisation they work for.

EMOTIONAL STYLE

	Green Button	Red Button
Double Checker	Listen to their story or concerns without interruption Test ideas with them before introducing to the solution Asking how they get things done	Forgetting to thank them Introduce new or untried ideas Making light of their protestations of concerns

60

Double Checker Emotional Style

Primary Driver: Desire for Security

What to look for		To communicate with	To present and Close them
Language	Complaining, Critical, Pessimistic, Will find fault, Hypochondriac	• Help them get started with new problems	• Be honest about "Facts and Feelings"
		• Help them with a problem, don't solve it for them	• Offer guarantees
Ideals	Risk averse	• Keep regular "How you going" contact	• Use reassuring terminology (*Safe, secure, proven*)
Vocation	Administration, Long serving, Accounting, Welfare	• Provide regular, positive feedback	• Don't use the word "Decision"
Image	Earthy colours, Practical, Stodgy, Full handbag	• Treat errors or mistakes as a lesson not a criticism	• Assumptive close
Neatness	Filled with files, Family photos & Medications	• They work well in a team environment	• Be prepared for a long presentation (*Make a value judgement on whether it is worth it*)
Gambit	Early or Late & Informal	• Indecisiveness or tardiness is an indication they are stuck and need support	• Have all the facts available (*When facts are asked for, use the opportunity for a trial close*)

61

Emnome Worksheet

Consider the Double Checker Emotional Style. Identify a person in a current or past sales campaign who has influence on the sales outcome and which you think best summarises this Emotional Style. If there are others in your organisation who are involved with this person or campaign get them involved with this discussion as well.

Name :

Role :

What outward signs give you the clues about this person Emnome? You might want to use the LIVING table on page 91

1.

2.

3.

In dealing with this person have you pushed their green or red buttons? What happened?

_____

_____

_____

List three things you could do with this person to help build your relationship with them.

1.

2.

3.

CHAPTER 8

ARTIST EMOTIONAL STYLE

The Artist Emotional Style will strike you as significantly introverted. They will be reluctant to make eye contact and tend to speak in a circumspect and cautious manner using words like 'maybe' or 'perhaps'.

They take a long time to answer a question. Don't be too quick to offer further comment as they are still considering the best answer to your question. If you rush in to 'fill the silence' you are likely to experience their tendency to become stubborn and become overly sensitive.

The Artists primary drive is to *create* or be different. In fact, the Artist Emotional Style genuinely wants to make a difference. They really do care about the way the world is going. They are life's philosophers.

Unfortunately this means that they have not got a commercial bone in their body. If your product or service means that they will gain materially it will push their red button. To push the Artist's green button focus on the greater good, the difference your product or service will make to the company and the people that work there.

Selling to the Artist

When it comes to the decking or deck...

"Mr/Mrs/Ms Artist... This deck allows you to keep in touch with reality. Imagine coming out here first thing in the morning and just soaking up Mother Nature.

Again, we have a style here that is difficult to close. Consider the higher minded approach (Which I admit is difficult with this example).

The Artist Emotional Style is all about the higher minded issues in life. They are the true believers. They do make decisions but they have to serve an altruistic purpose. The good news is you will rarely run into the Artist style as they only represent a small percentage of the population and usually not in key corporate positions.

Working with the Artist

The Artist typically learns and communicates using pictures so your communication needs to trigger their visual senses. To do this use visual words in questions and conversation and this will prompt pictures.

Your initial discussion

This is likely to be difficult. You need to work at it, be persistent, and be prepared with questions. The Artist tends to have a small group of close friends and colleagues so to break into this circle can take time.

Here are a few conversation starters to get the Artist going.

- How do you see this role being filled?
- What do you see as the important aspects of this program?

- Why do you think the board sees it that way?
- Where will this make the biggest difference to the organisation?
- When do you see this happening?

When you ask a question pause and wait for the answer. The Artist may be forming a picture in their mind and you need to wait for it to become clear and then turn the picture into words.

As this is the first meeting you will want to avoid personal questions. Save these for the third meeting or at some social occasion. Questions about their desire to climb the social or corporate ladder may be awkward.

Avoid using the word 'No' or challenging an idea of theirs too hard. If you do need to redirect the conversation you could try something like 'Have you considered ...'.

Follow-up

The Artist needs written communication for follow-up. A nice hand written greeting card to thank them for the meeting with a motivational message will go a long way to building the relationship. Send an email outlining the discussion with the agreed points. Ask them to review the notes and provide feedback.

Do not spring a surprise meeting on the Artist. Always call ahead and let them know you are coming.

EMOTIONAL STYLE

	Green Button	Red Button
Artist	Allow initial discussion to be broad or philosophical if needed Discuss ideas openly and with candor Seek input / opinion from them	Loud or insensitive behaviour Placing them on a pedestals or over others in a team Ignoring or not allowing for their feelings or mood Creating or allowing conversation to become confrontational

Artist Emotional Style

Primary Driver: Desire to Create

What to look for		To communicate with	To present and Close them
Language	Bashful, Quiet, Avoids eye contact, Hand over mouth	• Any feedback, positive or negative, needs to be given in private	• Explain how your product / service helps people
		• Ask questions and wait, then wait longer. Don't interrupt as they will eventually answer	• Don't force eye contact
Ideals	Creative		• Don't talk fast or loud
Vocation	Creative / Design	• Keep your conversation low key	• Use "Impending Event" close
Image	Unusual ties, Stylish or designer cloths.	• Minimise face to face contact unless otherwise invited	• Paint "Word" pictures
	Women: Long hair & big earrings	• Communicate by way of memoranda or notes	• When presenting the feature / benefits, emphasise people oriented benefits
	Men:- Beard	• They work better tucked away alone	• Never offer a discount or suggest a "Deal"
Neatness	Original artwork, Desk facing away from the door, designer furniture		
Gambit	On time & Formal		

Emnome Worksheet

Consider the Artist Emotional Style. Identify a person in a current or past sales campaign who has influence on the sales outcome and which you think best summarises this Emotional Style. If there are others in your organisation who are involved with this person or campaign get them involved with this discussion as well.

Name :

Role :

What outward signs give you the clues about this person Emnome? You might want to use the LIVING table on page 91.

2.

3.

In dealing with this person have you pushed their green or red buttons? What happened?

_____

_____

_____

List three things you could do with this person to help build your relationship with them.

1.

2.

3.

CHAPTER 9

POLITICIAN EMOTIONAL STYLE

The Politician Emotional Style is usually in a management or decision making role so a sales person is likely to have to contend with this style more than most.

They are opinionated, if not arrogant, and they will attempt to force you to get to the bottom line as quickly as possible. This is just their way of barrelling/bulldozing you out the door as quickly as possible.

You can do one of two things, you either accommodate them and start talking feature/benefits at a rapid pace or...you can take over the presentation, moderate your pace (slow down) and start asking pertinent/probing questions.

These people do not suffer fools easily and their sales resistance is likened to a boxer in the first round who has only got one big punch (intimidation).

If you allow yourself to go on the defensive and back peddle around the sales ring you push their red button and they will treat you with contempt. However, if you stand your ground you will push their green button and they will respect you, begin to listen and appreciate your comments. Remember, the first person who blinks ....losses.

The Politicians' primary drive is to *win*. Unfortunately, their version of winning is usually at the expense of everyone around them. The advantage you have once you recognise the Style you are dealing with is that you can use the simplest reverse psychology to control the sales situation.

Selling to the Politician

When it comes to the decking or deck...

"Mr/Mrs/Ms Politician... Frankly Mr/Mrs/Ms Politician this decking makes it one of the best properties in the area. Are you confident it is well within your price bracket?

This comment and others like it are designed to accommodate or provoke the Politicians need to win.

If you show any sign of sycophantic behaviour or you are unnecessarily obliging, they will simply dismiss you and anything you may have to offer. If you show some backbone and stand your ground they will respect you and most likely give you a hearing.

I am not advocating that you argue with this prospect, just state your position in positive but firm terms. To a large degree you are simply, mirroring the better side of the Politicians natural behaviour.

These people are usually driven by a need to succeed and they pride themselves on their desire and need for excellence.

One further note: If you are late for your appointment ...you are dead!

Working with the Politician

The Politician typically learns and communicates using words so communication needs to be auditory. Words are important to them so be prepared with your questions. If there are words specific to their industry you need to be able to pronounce them correctly as a poorly spoken word will get you offside.

Your initial discussion

Getting the appointment is probably just as hard as the conversation. You need to come out of the blocks quickly with your prepared questions. Here are a few conversation starters to get the Politician going.

- How does this role sound to you?
- What would you say are the important aspects of this program?
- Have you heard people talking about how your competitors are using this program?
- Tell me how this will make a difference to your organisation?
- Where did the talk about the problems first start?

To plant new ideas, it is best to allow the Politician to discover the solution and let them promote it. Questions like 'Have you considered ...' or, 'Perhaps it could work like ...' can be used to plant ideas.

The Politician wants to know how your idea or proposal will increase their standing or position of power. Use their name regularly in conversation and focus the discussion in the proposal on them and their importance.

As this is the first meeting personal questions are fine. You just need to be sure you get to the point quickly as the Politician values words and does not appreciate words being used too frivolously. Using the word 'No' is fine if you really mean no. Feel free to push back on their ideas and defend your position. You will win points if you have a valid point. 'We tried that with John Smith Company and it didn't work like we planned. I think this way will give you the results you are after and place you and your company back in the number one position'.

Follow-up

If you have used questions to plant ideas follow-up with articles from well regarded publications with a hand written note saying, 'Here is someone trying the idea we discussed'. This will help water the idea allowing you to follow this up in a few days.

Be prepared for delays in responses to email and telephone calls and allow them to call you out of business hours.

The Politician is always busy. Make appointments well in advance and expect them to be late or postpone or cancel the meeting at the last minute.

EMOTIONAL STYLE

	Green Button	Red Button
Politician	Show how your idea will help them win / look good Talk using personal words like 'you' To the point & ready for action Maintain a high level of eye contact	Telling them what they can or cannot do Being indecisive or not having a way forward Taking advantage of them

Politician Emotional Style

Primary Driver: Desire to Win

What to look for		To communicate with	To present and Close them
Language	I-I-I, Boastful, Opinionated, Forceful, Articulate	• If you ask for input they respond well • Acknowledge and success publicly	• Don't get into an argument … you will loose (*even if you are right*) • Politicians despise sycophantic behaviour (*Show some backbone*)
Ideals	Powerful		
Vocation	General Management	• Criticism needs to be done in private	• Be firm but polite
Image	Conservative, High Quality, Impressive, Blue	• Base criticisms on fact, not opinion • Focus on them providing solutions	• Show how your product / service will make them look good
Neatness	Dominant Desk, Degrees, Plaques & Awards, Impressive	• Do not argue or get involved in rationalisations, Continue to seek solutions	• Use their decisiveness to close (*"You strike me as a person who can make a decision"*)
Gambit	Late & Formal	• Find points of agreement and use them as a base for difficult topics • As a last resort, force the issue	• Use the "Alternative" close (*Do you want the red one or the blue*) • Be persistent

Emnome Worksheet

Consider the Politician Emotional Style. Identify a person in a current or past sales campaign who has influence on the sales outcome and which you think best summarises this Emotional Style. If there are others in your organisation who are involved with this person or campaign get them involved with this discussion as well.

Name :

Role :

What outward signs give you the clues about this person Emnome? You might want to use the LIVING table on page 91

1.

2.

3.

In dealing with this person have you pushed their green or red buttons? What happened?

_____

_____

_____

List three things you could do with this person to help build your relationship with them.

1.

2.

3.

CHAPTER 10

ENGINEER EMOTIONAL STYLE

The Engineer Emotional Style will demonstrate themselves to be fascinated with detail and how things work. When you ask them the time of day they will start telling you how to make a watch.

If you are a no-nonsense, bottom line, get to the facts type of person (Like the Politician) you will find the Engineer very, very irritating. They have great difficulty distinguishing between the fundamental or basic facts that are needed in any given situation and unnecessary or superfluous detail.

It is very important to use trial closes as early as possible to establish whether they are interested in getting an education on your service or product or they are actually considering a purchase. If you can't make the distinction, you will waste an inordinate amount of time for no result.

Their primary drive is an intellectual/emotional need for *detail*. You find them in the sciences and engineering or any other field that requires massive amounts of complicated detail.

Again, you need to be sure they are genuine buyers and not just interested / curious on-lookers. These people actually read your brochure from top to bottom and they will pull you up if anything is not exactly correct.

Selling to the Engineer

When it comes to the decking or deck...

"Mr/Mrs/Ms Engineer... this decking has been built by a real professional. Let's get down underneath and have a look at how it has been put together."

Remember, you would only bother going to this extent if you have qualified their intentions.

Working with the Engineer

The Engineer is typically thinking in terms of actions. They learn and communicate by showing and doing so communication needs to be action focused. Use action and feeling words in your questions to get their mind going.

Your initial discussion

The Engineer is likely to be detached until their mind is engaged. They need to know why you are meeting with them and what you hope to get out of the meeting so having a written agenda is a great idea. If appropriate, ask them if there is anything else they would like to add to the list.

Here are a few conversation starters to get the Engineer going.

- What part of this project do you think you would like to be involved in?
- How do you feel this may change the way projects are run?
- Why do you think the board feels so strongly about this?

80

- Are you getting a feel of how this model will work?
- How are you feeling about the proposal? Hot? Warm?
- When do you feel this will happen?

When asking a technical question listen to the answer carefully. If you do not understand say something like 'How do you mean?' and they will continue the discussion. Unless you are an expert do not challenge their competence.

When meeting with the Engineer be prepared to spend more time than allocated. If they become engaged in the discussion they are likely to immediately start planning how the project will run. This is a double edged sword. As a salesperson you may think they are ready to buy when in fact they are just ready to have a long and detailed talk about the possibilities.

Rather than saying 'No' you might try something like 'That is an interesting way of approaching it. How do you think it might work?' This will give them the opportunity to talk themselves out of that approach.

Follow-up

The Engineer needs details. Send them brochures, articles and project plan ideas. Include a hand written post-it note on the brochures and include something humorous. The Engineer likes to make light of their work while taking it seriously at the same time.

Send an email detailing the discussion as agreed asking them to review the notes and provide feedback.

Check with the Engineer beforehand and make an appointment as they do not like having their projects interrupted.

EMOTIONAL STYLE

	Green Button	Red Button
Engineer	Allow them to touch, feel and if possible, leave a working model Show the detail and plan or be prepared to offer detailed responses Openly discuss options	emotional and pressing for decisions based on feelings Surprise visits & unplanned tasks Challenging their expertise or exposing your lack of expertise

83

Engineer Emotional Style

Primary Driver: Desire to Complete Projects

What to look for	To communicate with	To present and Close them
Language: Monotone voice patterns, clumsy gestures, Over kills with information, Garrulous	• Praise or criticism needs to be supported by hard facts • When allocating work, show what, when & how then leave it to them. Do not interrupt or check on them	• If you are able, use the "Puppy Dog" close (*I'll leave it with you to play with*)
Ideals: Project and task oriented	• Don't frustrate them by not allowing them to complete a project	• Use engineer words …. Plan, organise, trial & test
Vocation: Project management, Consultant	• Give them their own tasks – the do not delegate	• Be prepared to spend a lot of time with the prospect
Image: Conventional, Mismatched, Pens in pocket, Gadgets, Green	• Allow time for overruns	• Let them touch your product
Neatness: Project plans, White board, Work organised in bundle, shelves full of technical manuals	• Make sure you stipulate what you don't need included in a plan or project	• Use brochures – they will actually read them (*in great detail*)
Gambit: Usually on time & Informal		• Point out the technical aspects of your product (*remember – they love detail*)
		• Solicit interest through trial closes as early as possible

Emnome Worksheet

Consider the Engineer Emotional Style. Identify a person in a current or past sales campaign who has influence on the sales outcome and which you think best summarises this Emotional Style. If there are others in your organisation who are involved with this person or campaign get them involved with this discussion as well.

Name :

Role :

What outward signs give you the clues about this person Emnome? You might want to use the LIVING table on page 91

1.

2.

3.

In dealing with this person have you pushed their green or red buttons? What happened?

_____

_____

_____

List three things you could do with this person to help build your relationship with them.

1.

2.

3.

CHAPTER 11

DETERMINING THE EMNOME OR EMOTIONAL MAKE-UP

While the understanding of each individual Emotional Style or gene is great, in practice each person is a complex combination of each of the Emotional Styles. How do you go about uncovering and understanding the emotional make-up of an individual without a psychology degree and couch?

Let's first look at the DNA, the building lock of life. Every living creature on the planet is defined by the DNA sequence in their cells. Simply put there are only four amino acid molecules,

- **A**denine,
- **T**hymine,
- **C**ytosine and
- **G**uanine,

When combined together in different patterns these four building blocks make up all DNA in every living creature and account for the basic outward structure of the Human Being.

The Emnome

The human Genome is the sum total of all the genetic codes off a human being. In emotional intelligence the equivalent of the Genome is what I call the Emnome. The Emnome is defined as the total emotional make-up of an individual. The Emnome is made up of seven emotional genes which are the equivalent of the four amino acid molecules in DNA.

While the Emnome is made up of individual emotional genes, which we discussed in the previous chapters, an individual is a complex combination of emotions. It is easy to understand the composition of a single emotional gene. When we are dealing with people, however, the Emnome we are dealing with is sometimes difficult to interpret.

Fortunately, like the outward expressions of combinations of amino acids in DNA, there are outward expressions of what the Emnome of the individual is like. In DNA there are obvious outward expressions of its make-up. For example, an XX combination is a female while an XY combination is male. Most people have no trouble telling the difference. While many of us do not understand how the DNA works, and most of us are not medical practitioners, we are all familiar with the expression of combinations of genes. We see different coloured eyes, skin colour, and various height and body shape. We do not stop to think of the actual DNA make-up, however, we are acutely aware of their expression.

In the same way, when we meet people, we pick up on outward expressions of a person's emotional make-up and their personality. Like the outward signs for the physical expression of DNA we also have outward signs of physical expression of emotion. If we can read the signs we can understand the emotional make-up of other people. Understanding another person's emotional make-up or Emnome is the key to developing relationships.

There are six main outward expressions which help us understand the Emnome of an individual. The process I use to help me identify the strength of each Emotional Style is to consider six aspects of their everyday living.

Language   By listening to the words and expressions used by an individual. Do they speak fast and loud or soft and purposeful? Do they use highly emotionally charged words? Are they blunt and to the point? Each of these gives us an insight into emotional DNA.

Ideal	Understanding the organisation they work for, which organisations they volunteer for, their leisure activities and the things they are passionate about will give you insight into their emotional DNA
Vocation	As was understanding their ideals, understanding the role a person plays, or the position within the organisation they work for, volunteer for or organise will give us a better understanding of the emotional make-up
Image	How a person presents themselves or the image they portray tells you a lot about their emotional make-up. It's not so much the clothes make the man, more of the emotional part of a man is expressed by the clothes they wear.
Neatness	This could also be described as organisation. Where and how does the person greet you? Is their office cluttered, full of trophies? What about their desk or kitchen bench top? Their Car?
Gambit	This is what I call 'how the person plays the game'. Are they early or late? Did they invite you for a coffee or to their office? Do they ask deep personal questions straight away or talk about the weather? Are they on time? Are they Informal or formal?

With a bit of practice, and a little coaching, you can pick the emotional DNA or Emotional Style by their actions, the words they use, what their office or workstation looks like and what they wear. Practice is important as you want to be able to quickly adapt to the emotional situation during a sales call. When you have your lunch, travel by train or are sitting in a public place try to observe people that pass by, listen to their conversations and look at their dress and neatness. Use these to predict their primary Emotional Style. You can even do this with others. It is fun and profitable.

It is important to remember while a person will have a primary emotional buying style they will have at least one other style that may be nearly as dominant.

When we can understand these it is simple to understand the primary emotional drivers and put in place strategies to satisfy their emotional needs. When your client's emotional needs are satisfied, rapport is established, and you can move on to doing business.

To help pick the emotional buying styles before a meeting it is handy to understand that certain Emotional Styles are more likely to appear in certain positions. For example, in older established organisations (e.g. established publicly listed companies) the Political and Normal emotional buying style is likely to dominate at the upper levels. In a newer organisation with an innovative product (e.g. new airline) you may find an Engineer or Hustler at the head. A newer sales focused organisation (e.g. Mobile Phone or mortgage Broking Company) may have a hustler or mover at its head.

I find the easiest way to narrow down the field is to eliminate rather than wait for positive identification. I then test the remaining styles. With luck, and a bit of practice, you can identify the primary style within 90 seconds. The secondary styles may take a bit longer.

Living the Seven Emotional Buying Styles - Summary

	Normal	Hustler	Mover	Double Checker	Artist	Politician	Engineer
Dominant Desire	For Social Acceptance	For Material Success	To Communicate	For Security	To be creative	To Win	To Complete Projects
Language	Logical, rational, unemotional, precise	Money (early), good eye contact, name drops, charming	Lively, laughter, smiles, jokes	Complaining, critical, pessimistic, hypochondriac	Bashful, quiet, avoids eye contact, hand over mouth	I – I – I, boastful, opinionated, forceful, articulate	Monotone voice, patterns, clumsy, gestures, garrulous
Ideals	Professional	Middleman	People	Risk Averse	Creative	Powerful	Project-oriented
Vocation	Administration, Finance	Broker, Sales (often changes job)	Sales, Customer Service	Administration (Long-serving)	Creative/ Design	General Manager	Project Manager, Consultant
Image	Conservative, 'Old School Tie', Black, white & grey	Flashy, well groomed, gold accessories, red	Tousled appearance, fun colours, casual, collar undone & sleeves rolled up, yellow	Earth colours, practical, stodgy, full handbag	Unusual ties, stylish, designer, beards, long hair, big earrings	Conventional, high quality, impressive, blue	Conventional, mismatched, pens in pocket, gadgets, green
Neatness	Orderly, formal, neat & tidy desk, landscape on wall or portrait of founder	Glitzy, lavish, awards & prizes, entertainment area	Messy desk, bright signs & posters, meeting area	Filled with files, family photos, medication	Original art, desk facing away from door, designer furniture	Impressive, degrees, plaques & awards, dominant desk	Project plans, white board, work organised in bundles, technical manuals
Gambit	On time & formal	On time & informal	Late & informal	Early (or late) & informal	On time & formal	Late & formal	On time (usually) & informal

91

CHAPTER 12

TYPICAL ROLES FOR EACH EMOTIONAL STYLE

In every organisation there are different roles that are suited to different Emotional Styles. These roles, in mature organisations in particular, tend to be filled by people with an Emnome of particular profiles. I urge caution in using these examples before you meet the person, rather to help you understand the style of person you are likely to meet.

Some roles typically preclude certain Emotional Styles. A person might be hired into a role; however, if their Emnome did not match the requirements they would quickly become dissatisfied and move on. More importantly your customers might start to question the wisdom of your HR processes. As an example, if I knew an airline hired the Mover Emotional Style to maintain an aircraft I would probably select an alternative airline.

So, which Emotional Styles suite various roles? And more importantly which style am I more likely to encounter in these roles.

Sales and Business Development Role

In sales the Mover is often selected as the correct Emotional Style to hire. They are good at making a person feel great and establish great conversations. The problem is that Movers are likely to forget to ask for the order. They are emotionally satisfied that they have a new 'friend' and had a great conversation. The client ends up leaving feeling great about the person they met but wonder why they didn't buy anything.

You may think that a Normal could fill the account manager role. The Normal will put in the hard yards to make sure the account is well looked after, client problems are fixed and anything that needs attending to is done. The Normal may look for new opportunities for awhile but with the first few rejections they will wilt and their need for social acceptance will force them to only undertake tasks that result in positive feedback.

The Politician is the natural closer. They focus on getting to the point and making it happen – even if it is blunt and to the point. The Hustler is the Emotional Style that can see new ideas and solutions working and can present the ideas convincingly.

The ideal sales person is a combination of the Politician and Hustler. The Politician knows how to press for a decision as they relish even the most polite confrontation. Equally the Hustler is often able to read the situation and adapt accordingly. They have a natural ability to solve problems so they are good at answering and addressing objections.

Administration Role

The Normal may seem like the most efficient and effective person to undertake this role. However, as they seek self improvement and social acceptance their actions are measured by this emotional need. They are likely to go back to school to gain additional qualifications so they are able to come back and take your job.

The Politician may also appear as a person that could do this role – as in a manager or director of a company. They would, however, take actions that made themselves appear better and may cover up inconsistencies that showed they were not the very best. If they are in administration roles and not the manager or head of the department after six months they will resign to pursue other opportunities.

Having people coming and going is disruptive, expensive and counterproductive to any administration department and best avoided in the first place. Your job is demanding enough and any good Double Checker will tell you that continuity leads to higher productivity.

Engineers make reasonable administrators or project managers although they tend to become jealous of their own work and not delegate or share in projects or issues. Equally the Engineer tends to tinker with projects and loose sight of overall schedules and deadlines.

In the end the Double Checker is the ideal candidate for any administration role. If you have something that needs managing in detail they are the ones to make it happen as it should happen.

Logistics Role

The Double Checker may seem like the ideal person to undertake this role due to the administrative nature of many of the tasks. Their attention to detail and risk avoidance may seem to fit the role well. However, this very attention to detail and time spent dealing with trifling matters could easily bring them unstuck.

The Normal may also appear as a good alternative for the logistics role, and this may be the case if there is limited or no interaction with customers. They may appear uncaring and cold dealing with customer problems and deadlines. If a customer does not have the paperwork the goods may not move.

Engineers, as they make reasonable administrators and project managers, could easily fit this role. Their attention to detail, especially for more complex logistics situations, means they will find the work interesting where others may find it repetitive and monotonous. Their downside is their tendency to let schedules slip to allow for new tasks in a process.

In the end I would look for an Engineer with a bit of Mover and Normal as this will keep the warehouse moving and customers feeling good they are dealing with people with their interests at heart.

Customer Service Role

This is a very varied requirement, so I will focus on the inbound telecommunications call centre for this example.

95

No matter what the role, when you are dealing with customers the person must have some Mover emotional genes. The question we need to ask is "What other characteristics do we need to back-up the Mover?"

In the telecommunications call centre role you may think the Engineer who will listen to the customer and plan out a solution. They might have good technical skills and can easily explain ideas and concepts on the telephone. The downside to the Engineer is they can become frustrated with people when they do not understand straight away or they may uncover other irrelevant problems which distract them and the customer giving way to new problems.

In the end I would look for a Mover with a bit of Hustler and Engineer. They will engage the client, look for creative solutions and look for new opportunities.

CHAPTER 13

DETERMINING YOUR OWN EMNOME OR EMOTIONAL MAKE-UP

To help you understand your emotional style this chapter includes an assessment tool to help you map your emotional style.

This is a simplified version of a longer assessment used to evaluate the profile of an individual. It is important to understand this is a tool to help you understand yourself and not to be used to place a label on who you are.

On the following pages there are 21 pairs of word combinations or concepts. Each set may or may not describe you. You are to select the set of words or concepts which describe you better. In the following example style 1 has been selected in the pair.

Pair 1	Conventional, even tempered, formal	Style 1 ✓
	Commercial, realistic, financially astute, hard headed	Style 2

As you work through the 21 pairs of words or concepts you may come to some pairs where you think neither or both of the sets describe you well. You must select the set which you consider best describes you of the two sets of words or concepts presented.

While there is no time limit for this activity, it tends to present a more accurate picture if you respond with your first reaction.

When you have made a selection in all 21 pairs add up the number of selections of each number in the boxes you have selected. For example, if you selected the words or concepts with style 2 in three of the pairs you enter the number 3 next to the words 'style 2'. You should have a total of 21 selections and a maximum of six selections for the style 1 to style 7.

On the graph place an X in the column representing the number of selections you have made for this particular number.

Once you have completed the exercise turn to the back of the book where you will find the emotional style represented by each number.

Pair 1	Conventional, even tempered, formal	Style 1
	Commercial, realistic, financially astute, hard headed	Style 2
Pair 2	Commercial, realistic, financially astute, hard headed	Style 2
	Active, Sociable, Outgoing, Alert	Style 3
Pair 3	Active, Sociable, Outgoing, Alert	Style 3
	Constructively critical, careful, steady paced, Security oriented	Style 4
Pair 4	Constructively critical, careful, steady paced, Security oriented	Style 4
	Sensitive, visual minded, reserved, imaginative, idealistic	Style 5
Pair 5	Sensitive, visual minded, reserved, imaginative, idealistic	Style 5
	Direct, competitive, openly determined, verbally fluent	Style 6

Pair 6	Direct, competitive, openly determined, verbally fluent	Style 6
	Precise, detail minded, orderly, project oriented	Style 7
Pair 7	Conventional, even tempered, formal	Style 1
	Active, Sociable, Outgoing, Alert	Style 3
Pair 8	Commercial, realistic, financially astute, hard headed	Style 2
	Constructively critical, careful, steady paced, Security oriented	Style 4
Pair 9	Active, Sociable, Outgoing, Alert	Style 3
	Sensitive, visual minded, reserved, imaginative, idealistic	Style 5
Pair 10	Constructively critical, careful, steady paced, Security oriented	Style 4
	Direct, competitive, openly determined, verbally fluent	Style 6
Pair 11	Sensitive, visual minded, reserved, imaginative, idealistic	Style 5
	Precise, detail minded, orderly, project oriented	Style 7
Pair 12	Conventional, even tempered, formal	Style 1
	Constructively critical, careful, steady paced, Security oriented	Style 4

Pair 13	Commercial, realistic, financially astute, hard headed	Style 2
	Sensitive, visual minded, reserved, imaginative, idealistic	Style 5
Pair 14	Active, Sociable, Outgoing, Alert	Style 3
	Direct, competitive, openly determined, verbally fluent	Style 6
Pair 15	Constructively critical, careful, steady paced, Security oriented	Style 4
	Precise, detail minded, orderly, project oriented	Style 7
Pair 16	Conventional, even tempered, formal	Style 1
	Sensitive, visual minded, reserved, imaginative, idealistic	Style 5
Pair 17	Commercial, realistic, financially astute, hard headed	Style 2
	Direct, competitive, openly determined, verbally fluent	Style 6
Pair 18	Active, Sociable, Outgoing, Alert	Style 3
	Precise, detail minded, orderly, project oriented	Style 7
Pair 19	Conventional, even tempered, formal	Style 1
	Direct, competitive, openly determined, verbally fluent	Style 6

Pair 20	Commercial, realistic, financially astute, hard headed	Style 2
	Precise, detail minded, orderly, project oriented	Style 7
Pair 21	Conventional, even tempered, formal	Style 1
	Precise, detail minded, orderly, project oriented	Style 7

Calculation of results		Your total must equal to 21. If not check you have included all the selected answers.
Style 1		
Style 2		
Style 3		
Style 4		
Style 5		
Style 6		
Style 7		

Plot Your Graph

Use the following grid to graph your emotional styles then turn to page 105 to lookup the style represented by the number.

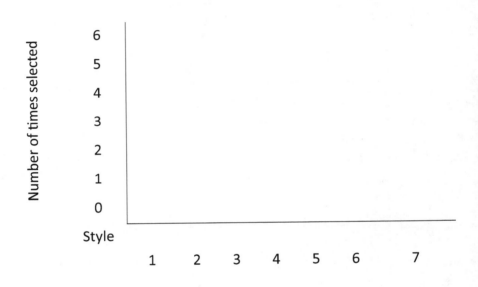

CHAPTER **14**

IN CONCLUSION

You do not need to become a Psychologist to learn to use the skills we talk about in this book. With this basic understanding and some coaching, you can pick the seven Emotional Styles by the words your clients use, what their office or workstation looks like and what they wear.

To learn more about these seven styles you can run a program called The Gatekeepers (see more at www.exceptionalsales.com.au) or ask for a short program focused on your sales team.

In late 2012 you will be able to purchase a training app for the iPad and other interactive platforms to help you develop your skills.

*Selling is an art
and it is an art worth practicing.*

TOP COACHING WITH OUTSTANDING RESULTS

Call to talk about coaching programs that deliver RESULTS - FAST! +613 9515 3322 or email us today at sales@exceptionalsales.com.au for details of our results focused coaching program.

Visit www.exceptionalsales.com.au for more information on Emotional Buying Styles.

Exceptional Sales Performance

5 Allnutt Court

Cheltenham 3192

Victoria

Australia

Tel: (03) 9515 3322

Fax: (03) 9038 4492

Email greg.ferrett@exceptionalsales.com.au

Table of emotional styles for the self test

Style 1 – the Normal

Style 2 – the Hustler

Style 3 – the Mover

Style 4 – the Double Checker

Style 5 – the Artist

Style 6 – the Politician

Style 7 – the Engineer

Made in the USA
San Bernardino, CA
30 August 2016